SWANAGE
& AROUND
THROUGH TIME
Steve Wallis

AMBERLEY PUBLISHING

First published 2013

Amberley Publishing
The Hill, Stroud, Gloucestershire, GL5 4EP
www.amberley-books.com

Copyright © Steve Wallis, 2013

The right of Steve Wallis to be identified as the
Author of this work has been asserted in accordance with
the Copyrights, Designs and Patents Act 1988.

ISBN 978 1 4456 1532 5 (print)
ISBN 978 1 4456 1555 4 (ebook)

British Library Cataloguing in Publication Data.
A catalogue record for this book is available from the
British Library.

Typesetting by Amberley Publishing.
Printed in Great Britain.

Introduction

In common with the rest of the Through Time series, this book pairs old and new photographs to allow the reader to see how Swanage and the surrounding environs have, or perhaps have not, changed. The old images belong, more or less, to the first few decades of the twentieth century. They generally come from postcards, which can be fascinating themselves in the subjects that have been chosen and the way they have been presented. I should add that the dates given for these images are estimates.

When taking the modern views that accompany them, I endeavoured to use the same location as the previous photographer. Various factors prevented this in some cases – a need to keep to public rights of way, a view now blocked by housing or vegetation, or in the case of one of the shots in Corfe Castle, the belief that standing in a main road to take a photograph is unwise considering modern traffic levels. In such instances, I got as close as possible while still getting a reasonable view of the subject.

Although the book's main focus is Swanage, I have chosen to look at a wider area in the south-eastern corner of Dorset. When looking out from Swanage, the Purbeck Hills form a natural boundary, and with one obvious exception I have taken them as the northern limit of the book's focus, with the western limit being a line running roughly south from Corfe Castle past Kingston. That exception is Studland, which lies just across Ballard Down from Swanage and seems like as much a part of the southern Isle of Purbeck as everywhere else included here.

The book is arranged by chapters, covering first the town of Swanage, then its seafront, before we take a little journey in both directions around the coast. The final three chapters cover a selection of the villages in the area.

When looking at the historic features of Swanage, the considerable influence of two people, John Mowlem and George Burt, soon becomes apparent. Before we start, I will give a little bit of background on them.

John Mowlem lived from 1788 until 1868, and like many local boys began work in the quarries, becoming a stonemason. He moved to London and eventually set up his own construction business, but retained his links with his home town, partly because Swanage was supplying much of the stone he used in London.

Mowlem's wife's nephew, George Burt (1816–94), also began his career in the quarries, before moving to work for his uncle in London, becoming a partner in the business in 1844. Burt took on increasing responsibility for the business as his uncle went into semi-retirement back in Swanage, and even more so after Mowlem's death.

Both Mowlem and Burt saw themselves as philanthropists and wished to benefit the town. The fact that ships need ballast helped considerably in this regard. The vessels that brought their stone from Swanage to London often returned bearing a variety of old structures that today we would consider important monuments, but which at the time were unwanted at their original locations, and in the process of being demolished. The two men bought them up cheaply, and once they had fulfilled their role as ballast, these monuments were then set up by Mowlem and Burt in various locations on their own land and around the town.

Acknowledgements

I would like to thank Dorset County Council for permission to take photographs in Durlston Country Park, and the Swanage Pier Trust in relation to the photograph taken from the pier.

The Town

Swanage from Ballard Down, *c.* 1925
We start with a broad view of much of the town and the southern part of Swanage Bay. This picture was taken from Ballard Down, which lies to the north at the eastern end of the Purbeck Hills. My photograph was taken from a higher vantage point than the old one, almost on the hilltop. Comparing the two photographs we get a good idea of how the town has expanded inland over the intervening years. There is a lot of new housing in the Ulwell Road area in the foreground of my picture, and most of the fields at the top right in the old view have now been developed.

Quarries, c. 1920

We head across the town and look down from the hillside beyond. The viewpoint of the old photograph is close to Bon Accord Road, near the water tower. The quarrying of stone has long been an important industry in Purbeck, and much of that stone was shipped out through Swanage, especially to London. The foreground of the old photograph shows how close the quarries once were to the town. Today this view is obscured by housing, but my photograph, taken a little to the west at Townsend Nature Reserve, also shows the remains of quarrying.

Church Hill, c. 1920
Descending into the town, we reach the High Street and find this little-changed view looking down Church Hill to the parish church. The cross at the top looks like a war memorial but actually commemorates Sir Reginald Palgrave, Clerk of the House of Commons, who died in 1904. A good selection of old houses lines the hill, some dating back to the seventeenth century.

The Parish Church, *c.* 1910

We drop down Church Hill for a closer view of the parish church, which is dedicated to St Mary the Virgin. Much of the tower dates from the fourteenth century, but the rest was rebuilt in 1859/60, and it was extended in the early years of the twentieth century. The buildings on either side are worth comparing: the eighteenth-century building to the left has undergone alterations, and the buildings to the right have been replaced completely.

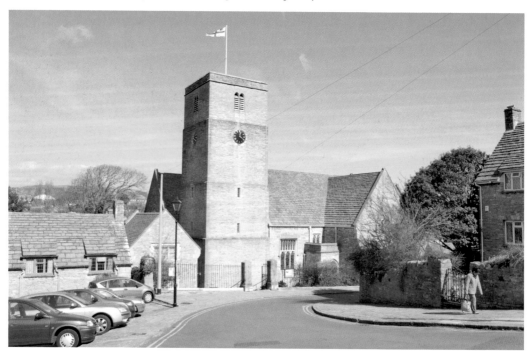

Church and Cottage, *c.* 1910

The cottage on the left in the previous view is part of a block of several that were built at around the same time, and some of which have been amalgamated since then. Here we have gone around the block to the left to find not just a lovely view of the end property and the church, but also the Mill Pond and the steps that lead down to it.

2267. Church & Mill Pond, Swanage.

A Lost Building, *c.* 1910

Moving a little further around the Mill Pond, we see in shadow on the left in the old photograph
a building that does not survive today. It looks like an outbuilding of the cottage we have been
looking at. We also get a clearer view of the Mill Pond itself, which used to serve a watermill, built
in 1754. This building survives but is out of shot to the left of this view. The wall around the Mill
Pond was probably built at around the same time as the watermill.

Old Mill Pond, Swanage

Further Round, c. 1905

We move a similar distance in the same direction, and again we see the since-demolished building on the left of the old photograph. This one also gives us a view back up Church Hill, and on the right there is a large three-storey building that no longer survives today. I might have guessed that it had an industrial function, but the line of washing suggests it was lived in!

Looking Back Across the Mill Pond, *c.* 1925

We go back around the Mill Pond and look over to the cottages that were behind us at the previous viewpoints. The three on the left are of a similar design and must have been built at the same time. I like the way that a house has been designed to fill the gap that we see in the old photograph without looking like an intrusion.

Wesley's Cottage, c. 1905

Back on the High Street, we head towards the seafront. John Wesley, the founder of Methodism, came to Swanage three times: in 1774, 1776 and 1787. On the first occasion, on the night of 12 October to be exact, he stayed in this cottage on the north side of the street. It was damaged in a German air raid on 14 May 1941 and had to be demolished soon after. My picture shows the inscribed stone on the street frontage that records the presence of Wesley's Cottage, and which suggests that he also stayed here in 1787.

High Street, Swanage.

KING.

The Town Hall, *c.* 1905

The next viewpoint is in the High Street opposite where Wesley's Cottage stood, and we are looking seaward. Here we find the first of the structures mentioned in the introduction, brought to Swanage from London by Mowlem and Burt. The tall building on the left is the Town Hall, which was built in 1880 by the Weymouth architect George Crickmay. The whole frontage of the building, however, formerly belonged to the Mercers' Hall in Cheapside, and was built in 1668 by an architect called Edward Jarman.

More of Crickmay's Work, *c.* 1910

Moving a short distance along the High Street and turning around, we again see the Town Hall, recognisable by the projecting clock, and two other buildings designed by George Crickmay. The terrace of shops on the right was built by him in 1877, while the ornate building in the background, which is now the Purbeck House Hotel, was built two years previously as George Burt's home.

Park Road, *c.* 1905

Our final view in the town might almost be considered suburban. Swanage's rise as a tourist resort in the later nineteenth century led to its expansion. Some of the wealthiest developments were beside new roads and streets to the south-east of the old centre, where the rising ground gave the inhabitants fine views across Swanage Bay, to which we head next.

Swanage Bay

45449. SWANAGE, FROM N.E.

Looking West from Near Peveril Point, *c.* **1910**

In this chapter we will use the old pictures as a guide as we head clockwise around Swanage Bay, and then turn and head back. This first viewpoint is only a few yards from Peveril Point at the south-eastern extremity of the bay. The tall and intriguing structure in the distance is the clock tower, and we need to get a closer look.

45450. SWANAGE; GENERAL VIEW, HILLS & PIER.

The Clock Tower, *c.* 1910

This is another of the structures brought here from London by Mowlem and Burt. It was a memorial to the recently deceased Duke of Wellington, erected in 1854 on the southern approach to London Bridge. However, it became a hindrance to the increased traffic that used the bridge, and by 1867 it had been taken down and handed over to the Swanage entrepreneurs. In the old photograph there is also a good view of the pier, which will be discussed later.

The Grove/Grosvenor Hotel, *c.* 1935

Next we go up the slope for a view of an area a little further around the bay. The large property near the centre of the old picture was built in 1838 and called The Grove. It was extended around the beginning of the twentieth century and became at first the Grove Hotel, then the Grosvenor Hotel. Further extensions took place during the twentieth century, and it was a much larger hotel that was demolished in 1988. In my photograph, you can just see the tops of some of the properties in the development that replaced it.

A Closer View, *c.* 1935

We move closer to the hotel in this old view. My picture shows two stone columns that were once in the hotel's forecourt. They were moved a short distance to Prince Albert Gardens when the hotel was demolished. The columns may look Ancient Greek (they are in the Ionic style) but they were only made a couple of hundred years ago, and again they were brought here from London.

The Pier, *c.* 1910

Next we head down to the pier. Look at the old view and you will see that it branches into two. The right-hand branch was the original pier, built in 1859/60 to load locally quarried stone onto ships. In 1874 George Burt started a steamer service from here to Bournemouth and Poole, and the resulting increase in visitors not only encouraged the growth of Swanage as a holiday resort, but also required the construction of a new pier in the 1890s. Although the original pier has since been demolished, you can just make out some of its timber posts in my photograph.

Pier Entrance, c. 1920

Here is the landward end of the pier from the other side, and we see that the two booths at the entrance survive today. To continue the pier's story, parts of it were removed during the Second World War to prevent its use by German invaders. Pleasure steamers used the pier until 1966, after which it went into decline. In 1993 the Swanage Pier Trust began its restoration, and continues to care for the structure today.

A Changed View, *c.* 1910
Moving closer to the pier, in the modern view, we see the roof of an outbuilding of the sailing club next door. Peering over this, it is good to see that an original lamppost survives.

The View from the Pier, *c.* 1920
A short way along the pier, we look towards the town. The tall terrace of brick houses to the left of centre is The Parade, and near the middle of the view there is a stone jetty that was a smaller predecessor of this pier.

Miniature Golf, c. 1925

Heading directly uphill from the pier entrance, we see this much changed view towards the heart of Swanage. The old picture shows that much of the hillside was in agricultural use in the early years of the twentieth century, although there is a miniature golf course lower down. Today most of this area is used for car parking.

The Old Customs House, *c.* 1935

This old photograph was probably taken about a decade after the previous one, from a location a little higher up and further inland. This time you can see people playing on the golf course. The prominent building beyond in the old view (but obscured by a tree in mine) was built in around 1830 as a customs house and library by William Morton Pitt. He was a local landowner, MP and philanthropist who made an early attempt to turn Swanage into a seaside resort.

Stone Jetty, *c.* 1920
Back down on the seashore, the stone jetty that we saw from the pier is on the left. This and the adjacent section of the sea wall were built in 1825, again by William Morton Pitt, for use by the local stone export and fishing industries.

North Bay, Swanage.

Shore Road, c. 1905

Next we take quite a leap around the bay to see the changes taking place in the early part of the twentieth century in a single area, with the aid of following three old views. The location is centred on the junction of Victoria Avenue (coming in from the left here) and Shore Road, which runs beside the Esplanade. This Edwardian view shows horse-drawn vehicles, bathing machines on the beach and seemingly unkempt vegetation on the slopes inland from Shore Road.

Booths Appear, *c.* 1920

I believe we have now moved to a time soon after the First World War. The bathing machines have gone, replaced by what look like canvas booths at the top of the beach, presumably for changing, sheltering from the sun, and so on. Also, the more permanent shelter has appeared opposite Victoria Avenue. Closer to our viewpoint, there are some larger changing huts, and the ground behind them has clearly been landscaped.

More Changes, *c.* 1935

Moving a little closer, the path in the foreground of the old view is the one we see today, although the huts have disappeared, for a while at least. Across the road, the canvas booths have gone, replaced by wooden huts on one side of the shelter. Since this old photograph was taken, the shelter has gained its clock turret, and the groyne that ran out beyond the shelter has become a jetty or mini-pier.

In the Gardens, *c.* 1925
We move back a little for a closer view of the landscaped area. I believe this picture was captured between the previous two old photographs – the booths seen in the earlier image are still there, but the path is part of the same layout as that in the later one. As you can see in my shot, this path has been taken up recently.

Shore Road and Beach, Swanage.

Down on the Esplanade, *c.* 1925

At this spot just above the beach, close to where the previous group of photographs were taken, we see lots of people enjoying themselves on a summer's day. More prosaically, on the left across Shore Road we see the wooden huts again, although there is no sign of the canvas booths. Note how much higher the beach is against the Esplanade today.

The Beach, *c.* 1925
Moving a little further north, I think that the old picture was taken from the shelter we looked down on previously. This time we see some of the canvas booths at the top of the beach.

10   SWANAGE BAY AND BALLARD DOWN

Looking Over the Trees, *c.* 1940

The old postcard seen here seemed odd to me; I wondered why someone took a picture where so much is obscured by foliage. Upon investigating, I realised that the photographer had chosen a vantage point on a concrete shelter that lies past Victoria Avenue towards Walrond Road. This was a gun emplacement during the Second World War. Steps lead to the top, and my shot from the same location was taken before the trees were fully in leaf!

View from Another Shelter, *c.* 1930

We keep going and reach another shelter on the Esplanade, almost halfway between Walrond Road and Ulwell Road. The old photographer used this vantage point well to get a good view of the beach, including a mix of bathing huts and booths on the left.

Back on the Beach, *c.* 1925

A short distance further on, this old view shows not only more canvas booths, but also a good view of the late Victorian properties in the angle between Ulwell Road and the cliffs that bend around the north side of the bay.

Turning Around, *c.* 1930
To reach this, our northernmost viewpoint around the bay, we go beyond the point where Shore Road turns inland as Ulwell Road, and follow the walkway above the beach, past what is now the Bull and Boat Restaurant, to stand in front of the wooden chalets. The colonnade that we passed under outside the restaurant is on the right as we look back.

Reverse View of the Bay, *c.* 1905

Heading back south, past Ulwell Road, we go up to what are now public gardens for this excellent Edwardian view. It shows most of the town as it existed then, and the seafront round to Marine Villas just before the pier. On the landward side of Shore Road, we see the rather wild grassland, cut through by Walrond Road and Victoria Avenue.

Thirty Years On, *c.* 1935

Three decades later, another photographer chose the same vantage point and an almost identical field of view, allowing us to play 'spot the difference'! For instance, we now see landscaping on the inland side of Shore Road, including buildings in the foreground that were the forerunners of the chalets of today. There are also timber groynes on the beach.

South Bay, Swanage.

Down in the Scrub, *c.* 1905

Here is another Edwardian view of the southern part of the bay, taken from deep in the vegetation just north of Walrond Road. This time we can see a little further around the bay, with the pier appearing on the left.

SWANAGE FROM NORTH.

2/7868 JV

The Shelter Again, Late 1930s

We go on almost to Victoria Avenue to see the shelter opposite us once again. This old picture shows a similar extent of the bay to the previous page, and in the distance you can make out a large building above Marine Villas. This is the Grosvenor Hotel, which had probably just been extended when this shot was taken.

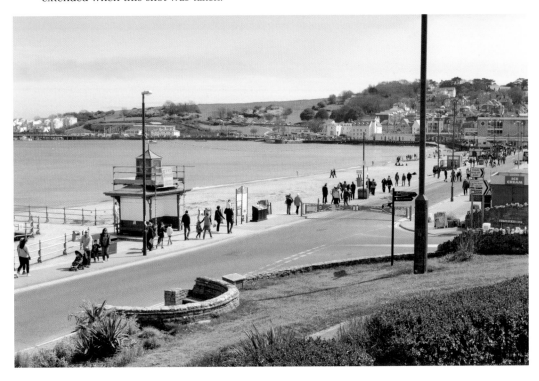

South Bay, Swanage

Bathing Machines, c. 1905

From a similar location, we turn to our right for another good Edwardian picture. There is quite an assortment of bathing machines on the beach, and at the far left across the bay we again see Marine Villas. Like the nearby customs house and stone jetty, these were built by William Morton Pitt, originally as 'baths, billiards and coffee rooms'. Over on the right of this view, we see the end wall of what is now the Sea Breeze Restaurant, and beyond it today's Tourist Information Centre, but nothing in front.

Public Conveniences, *c.* 1930

Heading across Victoria Avenue and staying on the high ground, we have a photograph taken a quarter of a century later. The end wall of the restaurant is on the right, and next to it the public toilets have now appeared, with the wooden huts we saw before on the other side of them. In the distance, we can see right out to Peveril Point beyond the pier.

The Southern Sweep, Late 1930s

Finally in this chapter, we have a good look at the south side of the bay, courtesy of a vantage point down on the beach. My shot was taken from the jetty by the shelter, and I believe the old image was taken from here or the groyne that preceded it. On the left you can make out the clock tower, while over on the right the Mowlem Theatre is noticeable in the modern view.

Around the Coast

Peveril Point, *c. 1930*
In this chapter we take a tour around some of the Purbeck coast, beginning with a view of Peveril Point, which separates Swanage Bay from Durlston Bay to the south. Here we look from the cliffs towards the coastguard station, to the left of which are the houses that were in the first view of the previous chapter. Coastal erosion and quite possibly coastal defence works have caused changes in the foreground of this view.

33705. SWANAGE: DURLSTONE BAY.

Durlston Bay, c. 1920

Now we turn around and head along the clifftop for a view of Durlston Bay itself. The old view looks from the top of the slope, where today there are houses, so my photograph was taken from lower down. We are looking across to Durlston Head, on which we see Durlston Castle, which today lies within Durlston Country Park.

DURLSTON AND SWANAGE BAYS FROM DURLSTON HEAD.

Durlston and Swanage Bays, *c.* 1930
We move effortlessly across to Durlston Castle and look back for a reverse view of Durlston Bay, beyond which we see the mouth of Swanage Bay with Old Harry Rocks on the far side. On the left side of my photograph you can see the modern development in the area from which the old photograph on the previous page was taken.

Durlston, *The Globe*, c. 1900

We drop down below Durlston Castle to see *The Globe*, constructed in 1891 by the local landowner, our old friend George Burt. This was designed to be instructive to visitors, in the way that Victorians thought was good for them. As well as the depiction of the earth, there is a panel at the base recording distances between the stars and planets, while more tablets on the wall behind give further statistics and quotations from the Bible, Shakespeare and other great literature.

Durlston, a Mystery, *c.* 1900

Here is another view of *The Globe*, which poses something of a conundrum. The large stone tablets behind *The Globe* are missing, and there seems to be just one small panel in their place. Like many old postcards, this one has been coloured artificially, but it does not seem to have been doctored in any other way. Unless the tablets were taken down for a period, it raises the possibility that they were set up some time after *The Globe* was put in place. My shot is a close-up of the panels in question.

49

Durlston, a Sight of the Castle, *c.* 1925

Dropping down the steps below *The Globe*, we turn for a view that includes Durlston Castle in the upper left and its outer turret in the upper centre. The castle was built in around 1887 by George Burt and was intended as the restaurant for a holiday complex that never materialised. It now houses the visitor centre and restaurant for Durlston Country Park, and was recently refurbished.

The Lighthouse, Swanage

Durlston, the South Coast, *c.* 1910
A path takes us a short distance downhill from Durlston Castle to the viewpoint from which these photographs were taken. We have now reached Purbeck's southern coast and are looking west towards the lighthouse. The path in the foreground is called Tilly Whim Road, and today it takes many visitors to the Country Park and the Tilly Whim Caves.

Durlston, Measured Mile, c. 1935

Moving along Tilly Whim Road a short distance, there is a mast by the lighthouse in this old view, although not in the previous one, indicating its construction in the time between the taking of the two photographs. This mast is one of a pair that is aligned perpendicular to the coast. Together with another pair exactly one nautical mile to the west, these allowed a ship to measure its speed. Several trips in either direction were needed to get an accurate speed because of variations caused by tides and currents.

2229. ANVIL POINT, SWANAGE.

Durlston Lighthouse, *c.* 1920

We continue on for closer views of the lighthouse. The old photograph was taken from the cliffs, while mine was taken from the main path, not only because access to the cliffs is now prevented for safety reasons, but also because I would not have wanted to stand where the old photographer did anyway! The lighthouse was built in 1881, and today is valued because both the lighthouse itself and the residential block, stores and enclosing wall survive in good condition.

Tilly Whim Caves, *c.* 1925

It is surprising to learn that much Purbeck stone was once quarried directly from cliff faces, and looking back from the path leading up to the lighthouse, we see the evidence. These caves are entirely the result of such quarrying. The stone was lowered into the boats that would take it to Swanage with a wooden crane known as a 'whim', and the rest of the name suggests that a person called Tilly was involved in the work. Much of the quarrying here took place during the Napoleonic Wars, when stone was in demand for coastal fortifications, ending in 1812 when the threat of invasion was lifted.

Tilly Whim and Durlston Castle, *c.* 1925
This wider view taken from higher up includes Durlston Castle in the distance. George Burt encouraged visitors to his Durlston estate, laying out many of the paths still used today. In 1887 he opened Tilly Whim Caves as a tourist attraction, which was closed in 1976 for safety reasons.

Dancing Ledge, *c.* 1920
Around 2 miles west of Tilly Whim Caves, we find another feature produced by quarrying. Here the impact was on a larger scale, and instead of caves we have what at first looks like a bay in the coastline. The extraction of different types of stone has actually left two ledges and, as both photographs show, since quarrying finished the area has been popular with visitors, although care is needed on the path down and on the ledges themselves.

Dancing Ledge, Lower Down, *c.* 1925

We now drop down to the higher of the two ledges. At the further end of the lower ledge there is a roughly rectangular water-filled feature that is only partly exposed by the tide in the old picture, but fully in mine. This was a manmade swimming pool, about which we will learn more when we visit Langton Matravers.

Old Harry Point and Rocks, Swanage

Old Harry Rocks, *c.* 1925

Going back to Swanage, we travel around the coast in the opposite direction. Beyond Ballard Down, and effectively at the easternmost tip of the Purbeck Hills, we find Old Harry Rocks. Here the chalk of the hills is constantly eroding, producing isolated stacks in the process. This old view was probably taken soon after St Lucas' Leap, the gap to the left of centre, was fully breached for the first time in 1921.

CM 99   Old Harry Rock, Nr. Swanage.

Effects of Erosion, *c.* 1935

This next photograph was taken about a decade later, from a point a few yards to the left of the previous view. Note in particular how the two arches at the base of the large central stack have grown over this relatively short period. My photographs give you some indication of the changes since then, although they were not taken from the same clifftop locations as the old views; these have been lost to erosion.

15560. STUDLAND BAY - JUDGES LTD.

Studland Bay, *c.* 1925

We head about three-quarters of a mile directly west along the north side of the Ballard Down peninsula for this view of the southern part of Studland Bay. In particular, we see the South Beach and Redend Point beyond. My shot was taken a little further west on the clifftop, from one of the few points I could see through the vegetation.

17361. AT STUDLAND — JUDGES' LTD.

Studland Bay, Reverse View, *c.* 1935

We cross to Redend Point and look back towards Old Harry Rocks. Today this viewpoint is close to Fort Henry, the enormous concrete bunker built on the clifftop during the Second World War, and from which King George VI, Eisenhower and Montgomery watched landing exercises in April 1944, less than two months before D-Day. Once again, I had difficulty finding a gap in the foliage!

STUDLAND BAY, DORSET.

91

South Beach, *c.* 1940

Next we drop down onto South Beach and again look back towards Old Harry. I am rather intrigued by the two-wheeled contraption by the right-hand edge of the old picture, and wonder whether it had anything to do with Second World War beach defences. Today there is a circular wartime pillbox on the beach by Redend Point – it has fallen down from a spot on the clifftop close to the viewpoint of the photographs on the previous page.

3669. STUDLAND: THE BEACH.

Redend Point, *c.* 1910

Going around Redend Point we get an idea of how it got its name, although the old picture has been coloured artificially and may not be an accurate depiction. Nevertheless, much of the sandstone that is eroding here has a reddish tinge, although there can be an amazing variety of colours within a single section of cliff.

THE BEACH, STUDLAND. 90.

Closer In, *c.* 1930

I believe this old picture is a closer view of the further of the two headlands shown in the previous image. It looks to have eroded quite a lot between the taking of the two shots, leaving it in a similar condition to today.

Studland, Looking Towards the Dunes, *c.* 1920

Turning around and continuing to head north for a few hundred yards, we see a very different landscape that does not seem typical of Purbeck. This is the widest and most popular of Studland's beaches, and inland the cliffs drop away to leave only the dunes and heathland that we see in the distance. Beyond them lies Poole Harbour.

Studland

Crossroads, c. 1900
We start a tour of some of the villages around Swanage at Studland, a couple of miles north of the town as the crow flies. The village is only a short distance from the cliffs and beaches we saw in the last chapter. Seen here is the central crossroads, where the lane to the parish church branches off from one of the oldest routes through the village.

The Same Again, *c.* 1935
This old picture was taken some thirty years after the previous one, but there seem to have been no major changes in the intervening period. Today things are rather different – the building in the background has long been demolished, the cart shed on the left has been refurbished, and in 1976 a cross was erected on an ancient base on the little grassy mound. In this case, my photograph is of that cross.

Manor Farm, *c.* 1900

We rotate our gaze clockwise around the crossroads. One end of the large building, which has since been demolished, can now be seen on the left in the old view. This end may have been two linked cottages, while the other end looked like a barn. The other building that we can now see certainly looks very different today – it has either been completely rebuilt or heavily altered. Nowadays it is called Manor Farm.

Turning Around a Bit More, *c.* 1905

Another small shift and we see more of the farm buildings behind Manor Farm. Today there is a teashop among these buildings. Comparing the angles in the old and new photographs makes me inclined to think that Manor Farm has been rebuilt, since its right-hand end is not in the same position in the two shots.

Parish Church, c. 1905

Up the aforementioned lane we find the ancient parish church, which is thought to date from the late Saxon period and was rebuilt soon after the Norman Conquest. Comparing the two views here shows not only some changes in the yew trees, as you might expect, but also that some of the old gravestones appear to have gone. In fact, I noticed that some of these had been laid flat on the ground in their original locations – a respectful way of dealing with them if they were in danger of toppling over.

Old Cottages, Beach Lane, Studland

a 220|108

Old Cottages, *c.* 1900

If you follow a footpath that heads seaward from the churchyard you soon reach Manor Road, with the Bankes Arms pub on the right. A little further past the pub you reach the site once occupied by these properties, which were much loved by photographers wishing to capture views of what they saw as typical antique Dorset cottages. I believe that they were demolished sometime around the middle of the twentieth century, although the wall in the foreground seems to survive, if perhaps with some rebuilding.

Another View, *c.* 1920

Here we have dropped down Manor Road to see the same cottages from the other side. You may have noticed that the title of the previous old photograph indicates that the cottages are in Beach Lane. There is no Beach Lane in Studland today, although there is a Beach Road a little to the north. Unless Manor Road once had a different name, I suspect that the publisher simply meant that the cottages were on the way to the beach.

Junction with Watery Lane, *c.* 1920

We now step back for a broader view of the cottages, seeing in the foreground a meeting of ways. Manor Road bends round and becomes Watery Lane, which runs to the little crossroads we saw earlier. In the modern photograph, you can see a track that runs off to our right. This heads down to South Beach.

Watery Lane, Studland Nº 8.

Watery Lane, *c.* 1920
The old picture has 'Watery Lane' in its title but, as I hope my photograph shows, I believe it was taken on the track that runs down to the beach. Although the track is not given a name on maps, it continues the line of the modern Watery Lane, so I suppose it was once considered a part of the latter. The stream that runs beside the track also makes Watery Lane an appropriate name.

Tubb's Cottage, *c.* 1910

We head back to the other end of Manor Road and its junction with Beach Road to see another very attractive little cottage. This 200-year-old property is now known as Beach Cottage, although around a century ago it was called Tubb's Cottage, presumably after a former resident.

The Agglestone, *c.* 1905

Well-preserved heathland extends inland from a good couple of miles west of Studland, as well as northwards towards the mouth of Poole Harbour. Pictured here is perhaps its best-known feature – the Agglestone, a massive chunk of sandstone on Godlingston Heath a mile west of the village. The two shots were both taken from the south-west side, but at first glance do not seem to show the same stone. The reason is that at some point it was deliberately toppled over, so that what had been the top is now facing us.

Langton Matravers,
Worth Matravers & Kingston

DURNFORD HOUSE, LANGTON MALTRAVERS.

Langton Matravers, Durnford House, *c.* 1905

In this chapter, we have a look around some villages west of Swanage that are linked by the B3069, which branches off the main road just outside the town. Almost immediately we come into Langton Matravers, and here we see the former Durnford School. This was a preparatory school opened in 1894 under a headmaster called Thomas Pellatt, who had the local quarrymen blast out the swimming pool at Dancing Ledge for his pupils to use. Since Durnford is now a private house, my shot shows that pool.

Worth Matravers, Village Pond, *c.* 1930

Two lanes branching southwards off the B3069 link it to the lovely village of Worth Matravers. Local attractions include the Square and Compass pub and the duck pond (*seen here*) in the middle of the village. Compare the old and new photographs and you will see that more houses exist today, but they blend in well with the older examples, as they are built of the local stone. In the old shot the top of the church tower can be seen in the background above the trees; they have since grown enough to obscure it.

49550. Renscombe Farm, Worth Matravers.

Worth Matravers, Renscombe Farm, c. 1925

The road that heads west out of Worth Matravers is popular with visitors heading to St Aldhelm's chapel and a spectacular section of coast. Many go on foot, although others drive to the car park at the road's end. At a bend in the road just before the car park lies Renscombe Farm, dating from the seventeenth century. The barn that is just visible to the right in these shots is of a similar age.

The Rockery, Worth

Worth Matravers, The Rockery, *c.* 1910

The area shown here is a real hidden gem. It took me some time to work out its location, partly because the name it is given on the old picture, The Rockery, is no longer used on maps. Today I think it is called Hillbottom. To find it, you follow the track that runs between Renscombe Farm and the barn in the previous view on foot. There is a locked gate with a stile to one side just beyond these buildings, then the track drops into a valley, and the houses we see here are on the opposite slope. The property on the left in the old picture is also on the left in my close-up.

Kingston, Village Centre, *c. 1930*

Beyond the lanes to Worth Matravers, the B3069 continues west along high ground before turning and dropping down towards Corfe Castle. The bend is by another well-known local pub, the Scott Arms, in the small village of Kingston. Turn off through the village and you see an enormous church (particularly considering the size of the place) built by the local landowner in the 1870s, and this view. The middle of the old shot in particular shows the village's Victorian water pump.

Corfe Castle

The Square, *c.* 1905

Whether you take the main road from Swanage or the side road through Langton Matravers and Kingston, this is where you have the pleasure of ending up – Corfe Castle. The old and new photographs here show the Square, with the cross on the left. The latter was erected in 1897 to celebrate Queen Victoria's Diamond Jubilee, and like the one at Studland it was set on the base of an earlier example. The buildings have changed very little over the past century, although there have been considerable increases in the numbers of visitors and, of course, cars.

Looking Across the Square, *c.* 1925

We move closer to the cross and turn to look across the Square. The projecting porch that is now near the centre of the view belongs to the Greyhound Inn, and on the right is the Bankes Arms Hotel. The latter was rebuilt in a historic style soon after the old photograph was taken, so that today it looks more like an ancient inn than it did then!

The Classic View, *c.* 1910

We cross the Square and turn up into East Street, the main road back to Swanage. Turning around we see one of the best views in Dorset – the great castle after which the village was named – and the Greyhound Inn with its distinctive porch. The wall of the parish church frames one side and some more historic properties frame the other. Please make allowances for modern life when comparing the old photograph with mine!

Little Has Changed, *c.* 1935

This next old photograph was taken about a quarter of a century after the previous one, from the road close to the same spot. The only obvious change over this time can be found in the vegetation on the houses on the right. These houses date from the seventeenth and eighteenth centuries. The Greyhound Inn was built in the seventeenth century as two houses, which were amalgamated in the eighteenth century when the porch was added.

Further Down East Street, *c.* 1925

As we look at this somewhat more distant view, it is high time to mention the castle itself. It was built around 1080 by William the Conqueror to guard a strategic gap in the Purbeck Hills, and it was extended at various times during the Middle Ages. Royalist forces held it during the English Civil War, and after Parliamentarians took it they deliberately blew it up to prevent its further use by their enemies. In doing so, they inadvertently created the picturesque ruin that we see today, which is now in the care of the National Trust.

Corfe Castle Church.

Parish Church, *c.* 1900

Here is the parish church, seen from the corner of the churchyard. As at Swanage, the Victorians rebuilt the main body of the church but not the tower, which in this case dates from the fifteenth century. The old photograph shows ivy covering much of the building – very attractive but potentially damaging to the structure. Note also the man in the centre, holding what looks like a spade, and posing for the picture.

46619. CORFE CASTLE.

On the Way to the Station, *c.* 1910

We move over to the east side of the village for a fascinating old view of the castle, taken from the road to Corfe Castle railway station. Presumably the flock of sheep was about to be taken to market by train. The railway also deserves a mention. Construction of the branch line from Wareham through Corfe Castle to Swanage was instigated to a large degree by George Burt, and it opened in 1885. In 1972 the line was closed and the track taken up. From 1975, though, the Swanage Railway Society has worked to restore the line bit by bit from the Swanage end, and today it is once again connected with the railway network.

Into West Street, *c.* 1920

West Street runs roughly southward from the south-west corner of the Square. Here we have gone down it a short distance and turned to look back. We see the tower of the parish church on the right and the castle beyond the Square. On the left we also see a good sample of the stone houses, many dating back to the seventeenth century, which comprise another of the place's attractions.

Further Down West Street, *c.* 1935
Going round a couple of bends, we continue along West Street and again turn around. The sizes of the castle and parish church give an indication of how far we have gone. Three-quarters of a century ago there were only scattered cottages this far from the centre, but today the gaps have been filled in. The property on the left is the same in both pictures, though alterations include the loss of the thatched roof.

Near the End of West Street, *c. 1930*
Now we head another couple of hundred yards further down. There are several eighteenth-century cottages on the right, and in the distance we have lost sight of the parish church. A little further on from here, West Street becomes a track across Corfe Common.

101: CORFE CASTLE FROM S.W.

The Castle, *c.* 1930

Corfe Castle is one of the country's – if not the world's – most picturesque castles, so I make no apologies for including a number of views of it here. The viewpoint for this pair is about halfway up what is called West Hill, but is really just the end of the western range of the Purbeck Hills before the Corfe gap. As at the parish church, we can see that a lot of vegetation once grew on the walls of the castle.

2916. CORFE CASTLE AND TOWN.

The Castle's Commanding Position, *c.* 1910

Going further up West Hill, we can appreciate the superb strategic position that William the Conqueror chose for his castle. It occupies the whole upper part of a conical hill that sits within this gap, which has always been the only easy route through the Purbeck Hills. The castle thus controlled the main road that linked Swanage and the lands around with the rest of Dorset, as well as the road to Church Knowle that we see here at the bottom of the hill. The bridge that carries the Swanage Railway across the road to Studland can be seen in the background on the left.

93

619   BIRD'S EYE VIEW OF CORFE CASTLE.

The Castle and the Town, *c.* 1930

Up to the top of West Hill next for a broader view. Though today we might consider the place a village, the settlement that grew up in the Middle Ages outside the castle had all the attributes of a town. Its original function was to provide services for the castle, and essential features such as the marketplace and parish church were constructed just outside the castle's main entrance.

CORFE CASTLE FROM CHURCH KNOWLE ROAD.   H. 4375.

The Foreboding Castle, *c.* 1925

Back down the hill we see the castle from beside the Church Knowle Road, with Vineyard Farm in the foreground. Enid Blyton loved Purbeck and based a number of locations in her works on real places in the area. Since this is the only castle in Purbeck, and perhaps because of the slightly sinister appearance that it can have, as in this old photograph, it is often assumed that Corfe Castle was the model for Enid Blyton's Kirrin Castle. One of her own letters, however, suggests she actually had a castle in the Channel Islands in mind.

Corfe Castle from Church, Knowle Road

The Castle from The Rings, *c.* 1910

These views of the Castle were taken from The Rings, which lie about a quarter of a mile to the south-west, again beside the Church Knowle Road. These earthworks are thought to have been constructed in 1139 by King Stephen, during the early stages of the Civil War he fought against the Empress Matilda, his cousin, for the throne of England. At the time, Stephen was besieging the castle, which was held by Baldwin de Redvers, Matilda's supporter.